Annika Sorenstam

By Jeff Savage

LERNER**SPORTS**/Minneapolis

This book is available in two editions:
Library binding by LernerSports
Soft cover by First Avenue Editions
Imprints of Lerner Publishing Group
241 First Avenue North
Minneapolis, MN 55401 U.S.A.

Website address: www.lernerbooks.com

Library of Congress Cataloging-in-Publication Data

Savage, Jeff.
    Annika Sorenstam / by Jeff Savage.
        p.   cm. — (Amazing athletes)
    Includes index.
    ISBN: 0–8225–2428–7 (lib. bdg. : alk. paper)
    ISBN: 0–8225–3107–0 (pbk. : alk. paper)
    1. Sorenstam, Annika, 1970—Juvenile literature. 2. Golfers—United States—Biography—Juvenile literature. I. Title. II. Series.
    GV964.S63S38 2005
    796.352'092—dc22   2004020232

Manufactured in the United States of America
1 2 3 4 5 6 – DP – 10 09 08 07 06 05

TABLE OF CONTENTS

Annika Sorenstam *(center)* and her playing partner, Dean Wilson *(left)*, smile as they walk the course during the 2003 Bank of America Colonial tournament.

GIRL AGAINST THE BOYS

Annika Sorenstam was nervous. She could barely stand up. Her knees wobbled. Her hands shook as she set the ball on its **tee.** Annika was competing in the 2003 Bank of America Colonial **tournament** in Fort Worth, Texas.

Why was she so nervous? Annika had played in hundreds of golf tournaments over the years. She had won many of them. Annika was the best woman's professional player on Earth. But this wasn't just any professional golf tournament. The Colonial was a *men's* tournament.

Annika keeps her eye on the ball as she starts her swing.

Annika watches the ball as it sails through the air.

Annika lifted her golf club over her head. She swept her arms down and through. Crack! She sent the golf ball whistling through the air. It bounced down the **fairway** and stopped rolling 243 yards from the tee. A perfect shot! And

A golfer tries to reach each hole with the fewest shots possible. So in most golf tournaments, the lowest score is the best score.

with that, Annika had become the first woman to compete in a men's **Professional Golfers' Association (PGA)** event in 58 years.

Hundreds of newspaper and TV reporters from around the world were covering the tournament. Thousands of fans were watching Annika play. Millions more were watching her on television. Annika does not like so much attention. She is very shy.

Annika plans her next shot as the crowd looks on.

The huge crowd watched silently as Annika attempted a **putt**.

But Annika was excited to play against male golfers. She wanted to test her game against the stronger men. Some people said she wasn't good enough. Some people complained that a woman shouldn't be allowed to play with the men. But Annika simply wanted to see if she could compete. "This is a way to push myself to another level," she explained.

With her next shot, Annika knocked the ball onto the **putting green.** Then she rolled a 16-foot putt near the hole. Annika tapped the ball in for **par** on her fourth **stroke.** The crowd applauded. One hole down, 17 more to go! Nearly five hours later, Annika's day was over. She finished with a good score of 71. "I'll never forget this day," she said, smiling.

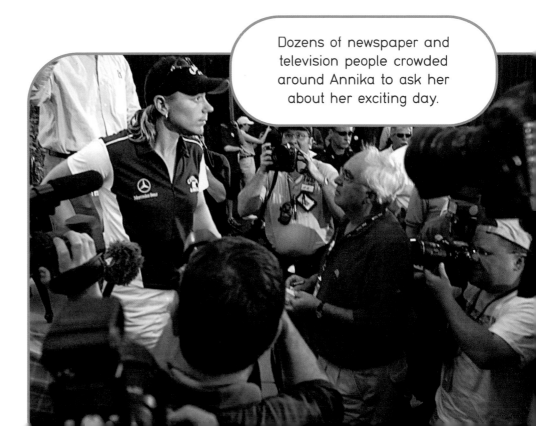

Dozens of newspaper and television people crowded around Annika to ask her about her exciting day.

Annika's hometown, Stockholm, Sweden, has warm summers and chilly winters.

GROWING UP IN SWEDEN

Annika was born on October 9, 1970, in Stockholm, Sweden. She grew up in the nearby town of Bro. Her father, Tom, and her mother, Gunilla, are fine athletes. Annika's younger sister, Charlotta, is also a pro golfer. The family played soccer, tennis, badminton, and other games.

As a kid, Annika's favorite sport was tennis. She didn't play golf, but sometimes she watched her father play. Her dad would pull her on his cart. Annika rode along with her dad's clubs. She pretended she was riding a horse!

As Annika grew up, she spent summers at a computer camp. She played ping-pong with her sister Charlotta and skied down Sweden's snowy slopes. She even dreamed of becoming a fighter pilot.

When Annika is not on the golf course, she is often using her computer. She writes e-mails and explores the World Wide Web. "Some girls are into clothes," says Annika. "I'm crazy about computers."

Golf is a popular sport in Annika's home country.

By the age of 12, Annika had become one of Sweden's best junior tennis players. But she was also learning to play golf. At first, she said she thought it was "actually kind of boring." But soon she learned to enjoy the sport. She liked being able to play alone any time. "In tennis you need someone to play with," said Annika, "but in golf I could go and hit balls when I wanted."

Annika joined a youth golf program. She practiced with 12 other girls. The other girls would practice for an hour after each **round.** But Annika always practiced for three hours. She wanted to be great. By the age of 16, Annika stopped playing tennis. She wanted to spend more time practicing golf.

Even in her teens, Annika was an excellent golfer.

COMING TO AMERICA

Annika's hard work paid off. In 1987, she became a member of Sweden's national junior golf team. Over the next few years, Annika played in tournaments all over Europe. She won many first-place trophies. At one tournament, she was sick with the flu. She even threw up on the golf course. But she still won!

In 1990, Annika received a **scholarship** to study at the University of Arizona and to play on the school's golf team. Annika was thrilled. But living in the hot Arizona desert was a big change from snowy Sweden. "I had never seen a cactus before," said Annika.

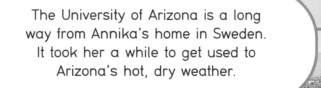

The University of Arizona is a long way from Annika's home in Sweden. It took her a while to get used to Arizona's hot, dry weather.

Annika proudly displays the trophy she received for winning the NCAA Championship in 1991.

But Annika soon adjusted. As a first-year student in 1991, she won the NCAA (National Collegiate Athletic Association) Championship. She was also named the college Player of the Year. She had a great second year too. In two years of college play, Annika won seven tournaments.

In 1992, Annika won the World Amateur Championship. She decided to turn pro. She left Arizona to compete on the women's European **Tour.** She did well, and in 1993, she was named the tour's **Rookie of the Year.**

In 1994, Annika returned to the United States to play on the **Ladies Professional Golf Association (LPGA)** Tour. The world's best women golfers play in the LPGA. Annika soon showed that she belonged with the best. During her first year, she finished near the top in three different tournaments. She collected $127,451 in prize money. Annika was an easy choice for LPGA Rookie of the Year. Yet Annika's amazing career was just beginning.

Annika kicks up some sand as she knocks her ball onto the putting green.

INSTANT CHAMPION

Annika was determined to get better. She worked hard to improve her strength. She jogged and lifted weights. Annika also did one thousand sit-ups a day. This helped her to hit the ball farther and improve her game.

Her hard work paid off in 1995. Annika had her biggest day at the biggest tournament of the year, the U.S. Women's Open. The tournament was held at the Broadmoor Golf Club in Colorado Springs, Colorado.

Annika started Sunday's final round five shots behind the leader, Meg Mallon. But Annika made her move halfway through the round. She made a low-scoring **birdie** at the ninth hole. Then she made a birdie at the tenth. Then the eleventh and the twelfth. Annika had made four straight birdies!

Annika made a string of great shots during the final round of the 1995 U.S. Women's Open.

Suddenly, Annika was in the lead! With four holes to play, she was ahead by three strokes. She finished well to win the tournament. She won $175,000 and a bright silver trophy. "It is a great feeling," Annika said, "a dream come true."

Suddenly, Annika found herself in the spotlight. People asked her to do TV interviews all the time. Everyone tugged at her for attention. As a shy person, this was hard for Annika. "I freaked out," she admitted.

Annika holds up the trophy she earned with her amazing win.

Annika cries tears of joy after winning the 1995 U.S. Women's Open. She had suddenly become a golfing superstar.

But Annika kept working hard on the golf course. She won four more tournaments in 1995, finishing the year with five victories. Annika won $666,533. She was named Player of the Year. This award goes to the best woman golfer of the year.

"It's hard to believe," said Annika. "But there still are a lot of things for me to work on. This is just the start of my career."

Annika watches her sister Charlotta *(right)* make a shot. Charlotta joined the LPGA Tour in 1997.

The following year, Annika won the U.S. Women's Open again. She finished the 1996 season with a **scoring average** of 70.47 strokes per round. This was the second-lowest scoring average in women's history.

In 1997, Annika blazed through the tour. She won six tournaments and earned $1,236,789—a new record. She also broke the record for scoring average, with 69.90. She was the first woman ever to average less than 70 shots per round.

Annika's success made her famous in the United States and Europe. She was a hero in Sweden. The Swedish government even put her picture on a postage stamp! Annika was thrilled with her success. "I'm walking on clouds," she said.

Annika has won more than 50 trophies in her LPGA career.

ALWAYS A WINNER

Year after year, Annika piled up the awards. In 2001, she set even more records. She won eight contests and earned a best-ever $1,506,209. Annika also won her fourth Player of the Year honor.

In 2002, she won a whopping 11 tournaments! Only one other woman golfer has won as many in a season. She collected an amazing $2.7 million in prize money. She also broke her scoring average record, with 68.70.

Annika's appearance at the 2003 Colonial was one of many great moments in her super career.

At the 2003 Colonial, she became the first woman to play against the men since Babe Dedrikson Zaharias in 1945. She fired a 74 in Friday's second round and **missed the cut** by four strokes. Of the 110 men in the tournament, Annika posted a better score than 11 of them. She told reporters, "I'm living the dream I want to live. I'm doing what I want to do."

Annika's trophy room is stuffed with awards. In 2003, she received the highest honor any woman golfer can receive. She was named to the **LPGA Hall of Fame.** Annika was added to a group of the greatest women golfers ever.

Annika's husband, David Esch *(right)*, often joins her on the LPGA Tour. They were married in 1997.

All the awards and praise pushed Annika to keep working hard. She kept up her winning ways in 2004. She won five tournaments, including one of the biggest of the year, the McDonald's LPGA Championship. She earned nearly $2 million.

Annika is driven by a powerful desire to be great. "I can't stand to lose at anything," Annika explains. "And I guess that's why I practice so much. What I've found is, life goes up and down. You have to keep sticking with it. One day when I no longer compete, I want to know I gave it my all."

Selected Career Highlights

2004   Won eight tournaments, including the McDonald's LPGA Championship.
Finished second at the U.S. Women's Open
Won sixth Vare Trophy

2003   Named to the LPGA Hall of Fame
Became the first woman to compete in a men's PGA tournament in 58 years

2002   Won record-tying 11 tournaments
Named LPGA Player of the Year for the fifth time
Won fifth Vare Trophy for best scoring average
Averaged 68.70 per round, best in LPGA history

2001   Named LPGA Player of the Year for the fourth time
Won Vare Trophy for fourth time

1998   Named LPGA Player of the Year for the third time
Won Vare Trophy for the third time

1997   Named LPGA Player of the Year for the second time

1996   Won U.S. Women's Open for the second time
Won Vare Trophy for the second time

1995   Won the U.S. Women's Open for the first time
Won Vare Trophy for the first time
Named LPGA Player of the Year for the first time
Named Sweden Athlete of the Year

1994   Named LPGA Rookie of the Year

1993   Left University of Arizona and turned pro
Named WPG European Tour Rookie of the Year

1991–1992   While at the University of Arizona, won the NCAA Championship and World Amateur Championship, and was named College Player of the Year

Glossary

birdie: to reach the hole in one stroke under par. For example, a golfer must reach the hole in three strokes to birdie a par four hole.

fairway: the grassy area that stretches from the tee to the putting green

Ladies Professional Golf Association (LPGA): the group that holds the tournaments of the top women pro golfers

LPGA Hall of Fame: a group of the all-time best women pro golfers

missed the cut: to be taken out of competition in a tournament because of having a score that is too high. The score, or cut, is set after players play two rounds of golf. Players must "make the cut" to get to play the final two rounds.

par: the number of strokes or shots that a player should need to get the ball from the tee into the hole. For example, a golfer must reach the hole in four strokes to make par on a par four hole.

Professional Golfers' Association (PGA): the group that runs tournaments in which the top professional male golfers play

putt: rolling the ball toward the hole by hitting it with a special kind of club, called a putter

putting green: the grassy area where the hole is

Rookie of the Year: an award that goes to the best first-year player

round: a complete game of golf, covering 18 holes

scholarship: money or other help given to a student to pay for college

scoring average: a number that describes how many shots a golfer usually takes to finish a round

stroke: hitting the golf ball with the club. A stroke is also called a shot.

tee: the area where golfers hit their first shot of each hole. Tee is also the name for the wooden peg that a ball is set on.

tour: a series of professional tournaments

tournament: in golf, an event to decide who is the best golfer

Further Reading & Websites

Armentrout, David, and Patricia Armentrout. *Annika Sorenstam*. Vero Beach, FL: Rourke Publishing, 2005.

Krause, Peter. *Play by Play Golf*. Minneapolis: Lerner Publications Company, 2002.

Simmons, Richard. *Golf*. New York: Dorling Kindersley Publishing, 2000.

Executive Women's Golf Association Homepage
http://www.ewga.com
This Executive Women's Golf Association (EWGA) website focuses on opportunities for women and girls to learn, play, and enjoy the game of golf.

The Official Website of the Ladies Professional Golf Association
http://www.lpga.com
The LPGA's official site has recent news stories, biographies of golfers, and information about tournaments.

Sports Illustrated for Kids
http://www.sikids.com
The *Sports Illustrated for Kids* website covers all sports, including golf.

Index

Photo Acknowledgments

Photographs used with the permission of: © Andy Lyons/Getty Images, pp. 4, 8; © Darren Carroll/Icon SMI, pp. 5, 6, 7; © MATT ROURKE/AFP/Getty Images, pp. 9, 26; Swedish Tourist Board, pp. 10, 12; University of Arizona Photography, pp. 14, 15, 16; © J. D. Cuban/Allsport/Getty Images, pp. 18, 19, 20, 21; © Nick Wilson/Allsport/Getty Images, p. 22; © Anne Hiles/Icon SMI, p. 24; © Vincent Laforet/Allsport/Getty Images, p. 27; © Sam Greenwood/Icon SMI, p. 29.

Cover: © Scott Halleran/Getty Images.